let's cook

thai

Christine
France

p

Contents

Thai Fish Cakes with Hot Peanut Dip

These little fish cakes are very popular in Thailand as street food, and make a perfect snack. Or, serve them as a starter (appetizer), complete with the spicy peanut dip.

Serves 4–5

INGREDIENTS

350 g/12 oz white fish fillet without skin, such as cod or haddock
1 tbsp Thai fish sauce
2 tsp Thai red curry paste
1 tbsp lime juice
1 garlic clove, crushed
4 dried kaffir lime leaves, crumbled
1 egg white
3 tbsp fresh coriander (cilantro), chopped
salt and pepper
vegetable oil for shallow frying
green salad leaves, to serve

PEANUT DIP:
1 small red chilli
1 tbsp light soy sauce
1 tbsp lime juice
1 tbsp soft light brown sugar
3 tbsp chunky peanut butter
4 tbsp coconut milk

1 Put the fish fillet in a food processor with the fish sauce, curry paste, lime juice, garlic, lime leaves and egg white, and process until a smooth paste forms.

2 Stir in the coriander (coriander) and quickly process again until mixed. Divide the mixture into 8–10 pieces and roll into balls, then flatten to make round patties and set aside.

3 For the dip, halve and deseed the chilli, then chop finely. Place in a small pan with the remaining dip ingredients and heat gently, stirring constantly, until well blended. Adjust the seasoning to taste.

4 Shallow fry the fish cakes in batches for 3–4 minutes on each side until golden brown. Drain on paper towels and serve them hot on a bed of green salad leaves with the chilli-flavoured peanut dip.

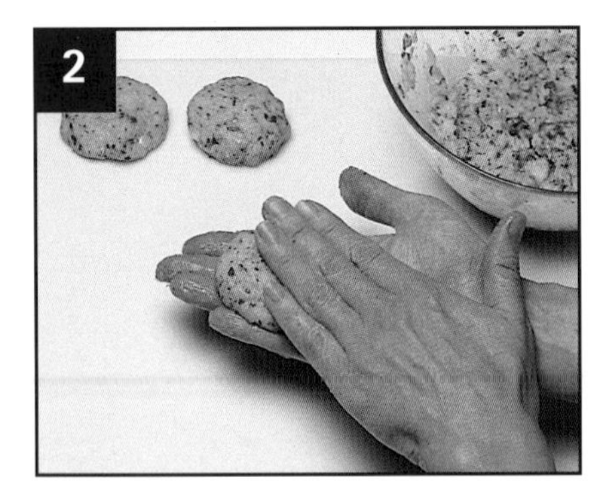

Roasted Spare Ribs with Honey & Soy

Ideally, ask your butcher to chop the spare ribs into short lengths, about 6 cm/2½ inches long, so they're easy to eat with your fingers.

Serves 4

INGREDIENTS

1 kg/2 lb 4 oz Chinese-style spare ribs
½ lemon
½ small orange
2.5 cm/1 inch piece fresh ginger root, peeled
2 garlic cloves, peeled
1 small onion, chopped
2 tbsp soy sauce
2 tbsp rice wine
½ tsp Thai seven-spice powder
2 tbsp clear honey
1 tbsp sesame oil
lemon twists, to garnish
orange wedges, to serve

1 Place the ribs in a wide roasting tin (pan), cover loosely with foil and cook in an oven preheated to 180°C/350°F/Gas Mark 4 for 30 minutes.

2 Meanwhile, remove any pips (seeds) from the lemon and orange, and place them in a food processor with the ginger, garlic, onion, soy sauce, rice wine, seven-spice powder, honey and sesame oil. Process until smooth.

3 Pour off any fat from the spare ribs, then spoon the pureed mixture over the spare ribs.

4 Toss the ribs to coat evenly. Return the ribs to the oven at 200°C/400°F/Gas Mark 6 and roast for about 40 minutes, turning and basting them occasionally, or until golden brown. Garnish with lemon twists and serve hot with orange wedges.

COOK'S TIP

If you don't have a food processor, grate the rind and squeeze the juice from the citrus fruits, grate the ginger, crush the garlic and finely chop the onion. Mix these ingredients together with the remaining ingredients.

Steamed Wonton Bundles

These little steamed dumplings are served as a first course with a spicy dip. It's worth making a large batch and keeping a few in the freezer to thaw and cook as you need them.

Serves 4

INGREDIENTS

- 125 g/4½ oz minced (ground) pork
- 1 tbsp dried prawns (shrimp), finely chopped
- 1 green chilli, finely chopped
- 2 shallots, finely chopped
- 1 tsp cornflour (cornstarch)
- 1 small egg, beaten
- 2 tsp dark soy sauce
- 2 tsp rice wine
- 12 wonton wrappers
- 1 tsp sesame oil
- salt and pepper

1 Mix together the pork, dried shrimp, chilli and shallots. Blend the cornflour (cornstarch) with half the egg and stir into the pork mixture with the soy sauce and rice wine. Season to taste with salt and pepper.

2 Arrange the wonton wrappers flat on a work surface and place about 1 tablespoon of the pork mixture on to the centre of each wrapper.

3 Brush the wrappers with the remaining egg and pull up the edges, pinching together lightly at the top and leaving a small gap so the filling can just be seen.

4 Put water in the bottom of a steamer and bring to the boil. Brush the inside of the top part with sesame oil.

5 Arrange the wontons in the top, cover and steam for 15–20 minutes. Serve hot, with a spicy dip.

COOK'S TIP

Make sure that the water in the base of the steamer is not allowed to go off the boil, or the dumplings will be undercooked and soggy. Also keep an eye on it so that it doesn't boil dry – top up with extra boiling water if necessary.

Chicken Balls with Dipping Sauce

Serve these bite-sized chicken appetizers warm as a snack, with drinks or packed cold for a picnic or lunchbox treat.

Serves 4–6

INGREDIENTS

- 2 large boneless, skinless chicken breasts (halves)
- 3 tbsp vegetable oil
- 2 shallots, finely chopped
- ½ celery stick, finely chopped
- 1 garlic clove, crushed
- 2 tbsp light soy sauce
- 1 small egg
- 1 bunch spring onions (scallions)
- salt and pepper
- spring onion (scallion) tassels, to garnish

DIPPING SAUCE:

- 3 tbsp dark soy sauce
- 1 tbsp rice wine
- 1 tsp sesame seeds

1 Cut the chicken into 2 cm/¾ inch pieces. Heat half of the oil in a frying pan (skillet) or wok and stir-fry the chicken over a high heat for 2–3 minutes until golden. Remove from the pan with a perforated spoon; set aside.

2 Add the shallots, celery and garlic to the pan and stir-fry for 1–2 minutes until softened but not browned.

3 Place the chicken, shallots, celery and garlic in a food processor and process until finely minced (ground). Add 1 tablespoon of the light soy sauce, just enough egg to make a fairly firm mixture, and salt and pepper.

4 Trim the spring onions (scallions) and cut into 5 cm/2 inch lengths. Make the dipping sauce by mixing together the dark soy sauce, rice wine and sesame seeds; set aside.

5 Shape the chicken mixture into 16–18 walnut-sized balls. Heat the remaining oil in the frying pan or wok and stir-fry the balls in small batches for 4–5 minutes until golden brown. As each batch is cooked drain on paper towels and keep hot.

6 Stir-fry the spring onions (scallions) for 1–2 minutes until they begin to soften, then stir in the remaining light soy sauce. Serve with the chicken balls and dipping sauce on a platter, garnished with the spring onion (scallion) tassels.

Vegetarian Spring Rolls

These bite-sized vegetarian noodle-filled rolls are a tasty starter (appetizer) to serve at the start of any meal with a sweet chilli dip.

Serves 4

INGREDIENTS

25 g/1 oz fine cellophane noodles
2 tbsp groundnut oil
2 garlic cloves, crushed
½ tsp fresh ginger root, grated
55 g/2 oz/⅔ cup oyster mushrooms, thinly sliced
2 spring onions (scallions), finely chopped
50g/1¾ oz/½ cup beansprouts
1 small carrot, finely shredded
½ tsp sesame oil
1 tbsp light soy sauce
1 tbsp rice wine or dry sherry
¼ tsp ground black pepper
1 tbsp fresh coriander (cilantro), chopped
1 tbsp fresh mint, chopped
24 spring- (egg-) roll wrappers
½ tsp cornflour (cornstarch)
groundnut oil for deep frying
fresh mint sprigs, to garnish

1 Place the noodles in a heatproof bowl, pour over enough boiling water to cover and leave to stand for 4 minutes. Drain, rinse in cold water, then drain again. Use scissors to snip into 5 cm/2 inch lengths.

2 Heat the groundnut oil in a wok or wide pan (skillet) over a high heat. Add the garlic, ginger, oyster mushrooms, spring onions (scallions), beansprouts and carrot and stir-fry for about 1 minute until just softened.

3 Stir in the sesame oil, soy sauce, rice wine, pepper, coriander (cilantro) and mint, then remove from the heat. Stir in the rice noodles.

4 Arrange the spring- (egg-) roll wrappers on a work surface, pointing diagonally. Mix the cornflour (cornstarch) with 1 tablespoon water and brush the edges of 1 wrapper. Spoon a little filling on to the pointed side of the same wrapper.

5 Roll the point of the wrapper over the filling, then fold the side points inwards over the filling. Continue to roll up the wrapper away from you, moistening the tip with more cornflour (cornstarch) mixture to secure the roll.

6 Heat the oil in a wok or deep frying pan to 180°C/350°F, or until a cube of bread browns in 30 seconds. Add rolls in batches and deep fry for 2–3 minutes each until golden brown and crisp. Serve hot.

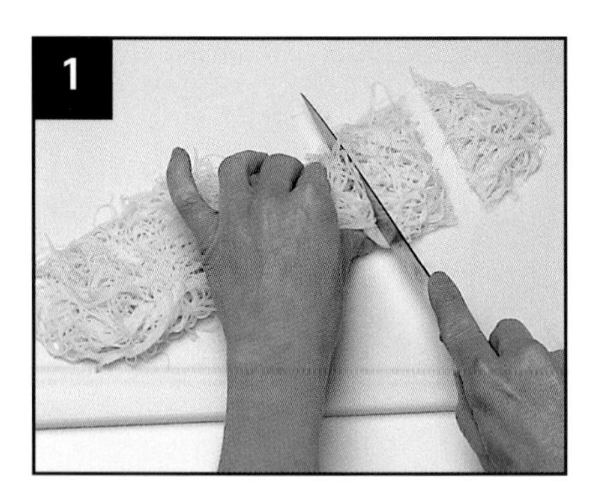

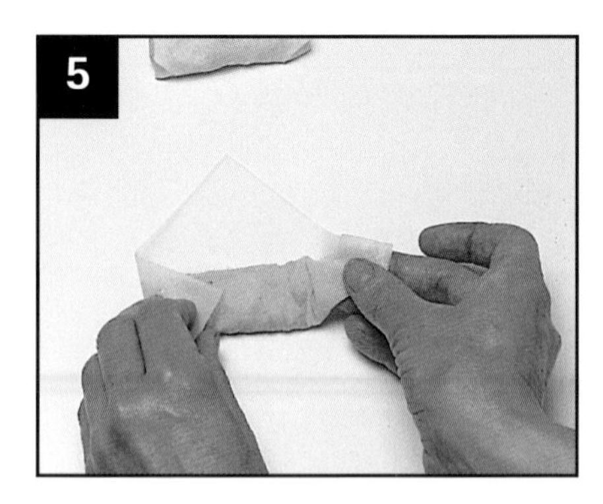

Hot & Sour Soup

Hot-and-sour mixtures are popular throughout the East, especially in Thailand. This soup typically has either prawns (shrimp) or chicken added, but tofu can be used instead if you prefer a meatless version.

Serves 4

INGREDIENTS

350 g/12 oz/2 cups whole raw or cooked prawns (shrimp) in shells
1 tbsp vegetable oil
1 lemon grass stalk (stick), roughly chopped
2 kaffir lime leaves, shredded
1 green chilli, deseeded and chopped
1.2 litres/2 pints/5 cups chicken or fish stock
1 lime
1 tbsp Thai fish sauce
1 red bird-eye chilli, deseeded and thinly sliced
1 spring onion (scallion), thinly sliced
salt and pepper
1 tbsp coriander (cilantro),finely chopped, to garnish

1 Peel the prawns (shrimp) and reserve the shells. Devein the prawns (shrimp), cover and chill.

2 Heat the oil in a large pan and stir-fry the prawn shells for 3–4 minutes until they turn pink. Add the lemon grass, lime leaves, chilli and stock. Pare a thin strip of zest from the lime and grate the rest. Add the grated rind to the pan.

3 Bring to the boil, then lower the heat, cover and simmer for about 20 minutes.

4 Strain the liquid and pour it back into the pan. Squeeze the juice from the lime and add to the pan with the fish sauce and salt and pepper to taste.

5 Bring the pan to the boil. Lower the heat, add the prawns (shrimp) and simmer for 2–3 minutes.

6 Add the thinly sliced chilli and spring onion (scallion). Sprinkle with the chopped coriander (cilantro) and serve.

COOK'S TIP

To devein the prawns (shrimp), remove the shells. Cut a slit along the back of each prawn (shrimp)and remove the fine black vein that runs along the length of the back. Wipe with paper towels.

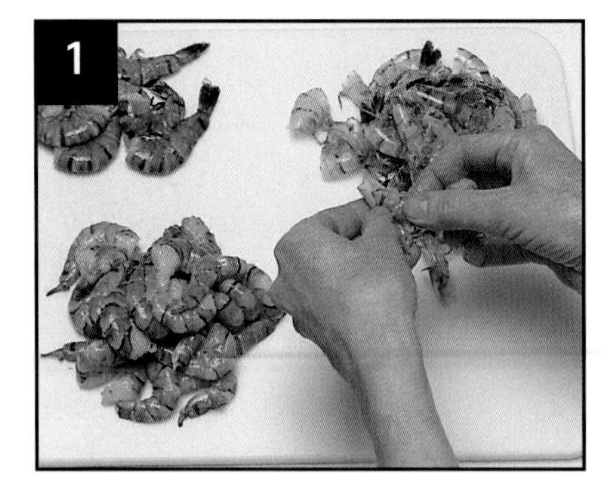
1

2

5

Hot Beef & Coconut Curry

The heat of the chillies in this red-hot curry is balanced and softened by the coconut milk, producing a creamy-textured, rich and lavishly spiced dish.

Serves 4

INGREDIENTS

400 ml/14 fl oz/1¾ cups coconut milk
2 tbsp Thai red curry paste
2 garlic cloves, crushed
500 g/1 lb 2 oz braising steak
2 kaffir lime leaves, shredded
3 tbsp kaffir lime juice
2 tbsp Thai fish sauce
1 large red chilli, deseeded and sliced
½ tsp turmeric
½ tsp salt
2 tbsp fresh basil leaves, chopped
2 tbsp fresh coriander (cilantro) leaves, chopped
shredded coconut, to garnish
boiled rice, to serve

1 Place the coconut milk in a large pan and bring to the boil. Lower the heat and simmer gently over a low heat for about 10 minutes until the milk has thickened. Stir in the red curry paste and garlic and simmer for a further 5 minutes.

2 Cut the beef into 2 cm/¾ inch chunks, add to the pan and bring to the boil, stirring. Lower the heat and add the lime leaves, lime juice, fish sauce, chilli, turmeric and salt.

3 Cover the pan and continue simmering for 20–25 minutes until the meat is tender, adding a little water if the sauce looks too dry.

4 Stir in the basil and coriander (cilantro) and adjust the seasoning with salt and pepper to taste. Sprinkle with coconut and serve with boiled rice.

COOK'S TIP

This recipe uses one of the larger, milder red chilli peppers – either fresno or Dutch – simply because they give more colour to the dish. If you prefer to use small Thai, or bird-eye, chillies, you'll still need only one as they are much hotter.

Thai-spiced Sausages

These mildly spiced little sausages are a good choice for a buffet meal. They can be made a day in advance, and are equally good served hot or cold.

Serves 4

INGREDIENTS

400 g/14 oz lean minced (ground) pork
50 g/1¾ oz/4 tbsp cooked rice
1 garlic clove, crushed
1 tsp Thai red curry paste
1 tsp ground black pepper
1 tsp ground coriander
½ tsp salt
3 tbsp lime juice
2 tbsp fresh coriander (cilantro), chopped
3 tbsp groundnut oil
coconut sambal or soy sauce, to serve

1 Place the pork, rice, garlic, curry paste, pepper, ground coriander, salt, lime juice and chopped coriander (cilantro) in a bowl and knead together with your hands to mix evenly.

2 Use your hands to shape the mixture into 12 small sausage (link) shapes. If you can buy sausage casings, fill the casings and twist at intervals to separate the sausages.

3 Heat the oil in a large frying pan (skillet) over a medium heat. Add the sausages in batches if necessary, and fry for 8–10 minutes, turning them over occasionally, until they are evenly golden brown. Serve hot with a coconut sambal or soy sauce.

COOK'S TIP

These sausages can also be served as a starter (appetizer) – shape the mixture slightly smaller to make about 16 bite-sized sausages. Serve with a soy dip.

Red Lamb Curry

This richly spiced curry uses the typically red-hot chilli flavour of Thai red curry paste, made with dried red chillies, to give it a warm, russet-red colour.

Serves 4

INGREDIENTS

500 g/1 lb 2 oz boneless lean leg of lamb
2 tbsp vegetable oil
1 large onion, sliced
2 garlic cloves, crushed
2 tbsp Thai red curry paste
150 ml/5 fl oz/⅔ cup coconut milk
1 tbsp soft light brown sugar
1 large red (bell) pepper, deseeded and thickly sliced
120 ml/4 fl oz/½ cup lamb or beef stock
1 tbsp Thai fish sauce
2 tbsp lime juice
227 g/8 oz can water chestnuts, drained
2 tbsp fresh coriander (cilantro), chopped
2 tbsp fresh basil, chopped
salt and pepper
boiled jasmine rice, to serve
fresh basil leaves, to garnish

1 Trim the meat and cut it into 3 cm/1¼ inch cubes. Heat the oil in a large frying pan (skillet) or wok over a high heat and stir-fry the onion and garlic for 2–3 minutes to soften. Add the meat and fry the mixture quickly until lightly browned.

2 Stir in the curry paste and cook for a few seconds, then add the coconut milk and sugar and bring to the boil. Reduce the heat and simmer for 15 minutes, stirring occasionally.

3 Stir in the red (bell) pepper, stock, fish sauce and lime juice, cover and continue simmering for a further 15 minutes, or until the meat is tender.

4 Add the water chestnuts, coriander (cilantro) and basil, adjust the seasoning to taste. Serve with jasmine rice garnished with fresh basil leaves.

COOK'S TIP

This curry can also be made with other lean red meats. Try replacing the lamb with trimmed duck breasts or pieces of lean braising beef.

Thai-spiced Coriander Chicken

These simple marinated chicken breasts (halves) are packed with powerful, zesty flavours, and are best accompanied by a simple dish of plain boiled rice and a cucumber salad.

Serves 4

INGREDIENTS

- 4 boneless chicken breasts (halves), without skin
- 2 garlic cloves, peeled
- 1 fresh green chilli, deseeded
- 2 cm/3/4 inch piece fresh ginger root, peeled
- 4 tbsp fresh coriander (cilantro), chopped
- rind of 1 lime, finely grated
- 3 tbsp lime juice
- 2 tbsp light soy sauce
- 1 tbsp caster (superfine) sugar
- 175 ml/6 fl oz/3/4 cup coconut milk
- plain boiled rice, to serve
- cucumber and radish slices, to garnish

1 Using a sharp knife, cut 3 deep slashes into the skinned side of each chicken breast (half). Place the breasts (halves) in a single layer in a wide, non-metallic dish.

2 Put the garlic, chilli, ginger, coriander (cilantro), lime rind and juice, soy sauce, caster (superfine) sugar and coconut milk in a food processor and process until a smooth purée forms.

3 Spread the purée over both sides of the chicken breasts (halves), coating them evenly. Cover the dish and leave to marinate in the refrigerator for about 1 hour.

4 Lift the chicken from the marinade, drain off the excess and place in a grill (broiler) pan. Grill (broil) under a preheated grill (broiler) for 12–15 minutes until thoroughly and evenly cooked.

5 Meanwhile, place the remaining marinade in a saucepan and bring to the boil. Lower the heat and simmer for several minutes to heat thoroughly. Serve with the chicken breasts, accompanied with rice and garnished with cucumber and radish slices.

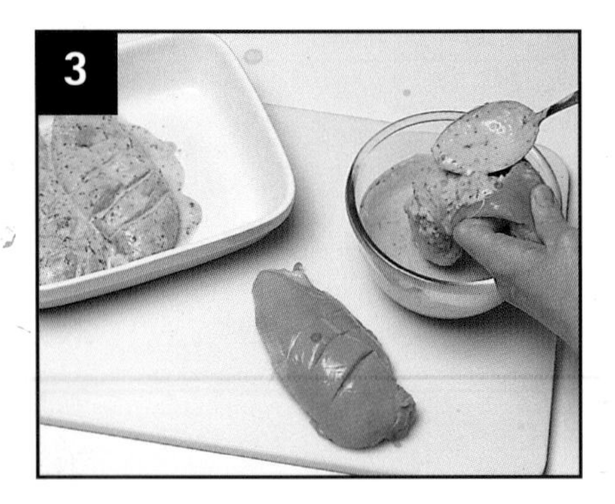

Green Chicken Curry

Thai curries are traditionally very hot, and designed to make a little go a long way – the thin, highly spiced juices are eaten with lots of rice to 'stretch' a small amount of meat as far as possible.

Serves 4

INGREDIENTS

- 6 boneless, skinless chicken thighs
- 400 ml/14 fl oz/1¾ cups coconut milk
- 2 garlic cloves, crushed
- 2 tbsp Thai fish sauce
- 2 tbsp Thai green curry paste
- 12 baby aubergines (eggplants), also called Thai pea aubergines
- 3 green chillies, finely chopped
- 3 kaffir lime leaves, shredded
- 4 tbsp fresh coriander (cilantro), chopped
- boiled rice, to serve

1 Cut the chicken into bite-sized pieces. Pour the coconut milk into a large pan or wok over a high heat and bring to the boil.

2 Add the chicken, garlic and fish sauce to the pan and bring back to the boil. Lower the heat and simmer gently for 30 minutes, or until the chicken is just tender.

3 Remove the chicken from the mixture with a perforated spoon. Set aside and keep warm.

4 Stir the green curry paste into the pan, add the aubergines (eggplants), chillies and lime leaves and simmer for 5 minutes.

5 Return the chicken to the pan and bring to the boil. Adjust the seasoning to taste with salt and pepper, then stir in the coriander (cilantro). Serve the curry with boiled rice.

COOK'S TIP

Baby aubergines (eggplants), or 'pea aubergines' as they are called in Thailand, are traditionally used in this curry, but they are not always easily available outside the country. If you can't find them in an Oriental food shop, use chopped ordinary aubergine (eggplant) or substitute a few green peas.

2

4

5

Steamed Yellow Fish Fillets

Thailand has an abundance of fresh fish, which is an important part of the local diet. Dishes such as these steamed fillets are popular and can be adapted to suit many different types of fish. Serve with a vegetable and beansprout salad.

Serves 4

INGREDIENTS

500 g/1 lb 2 oz firm fish fillets, such as red snapper, sole or monkfish
1 dried red bird-eye chilli
1 small onion, chopped
3 garlic cloves, chopped
2 sprigs fresh coriander (cilantro)
1 tsp coriander seeds
½ tsp turmeric
½ tsp ground black pepper
1 tbsp Thai fish sauce
2 tbsp coconut milk
1 small egg, beaten
2 tbsp rice flour
red and green chilli strips, to garnish
soy sauce, to serve

1 Remove any skin from the fish and cut the fillets diagonally into long 2 cm/¾ inch wide strips.

2 Place the dried chilli, onion, garlic, coriander (cilantro) and coriander seeds in a pestle and mortar and grind until it is a smooth paste.

3 Add the turmeric, pepper, fish sauce, coconut milk and beaten egg, stirring well to mix evenly.

4 Dip the fish strips into the paste mixture, then into the rice flour to coat lightly.

5 Bring the water in the bottom of a steamer to the boil, then arrange the fish strips in the top of the steamer. Cover and steam for about 12–15 minutes until the fish is just firm.

6 Serve the fish with soy sauce and an accompaniment of stir-fried vegetables or salad.

COOK'S TIP

If you don't have a steamer, improvise by placing a large metal colander over a large pan of boiling water and cover with an upturned plate to enclose the fish as it steams.

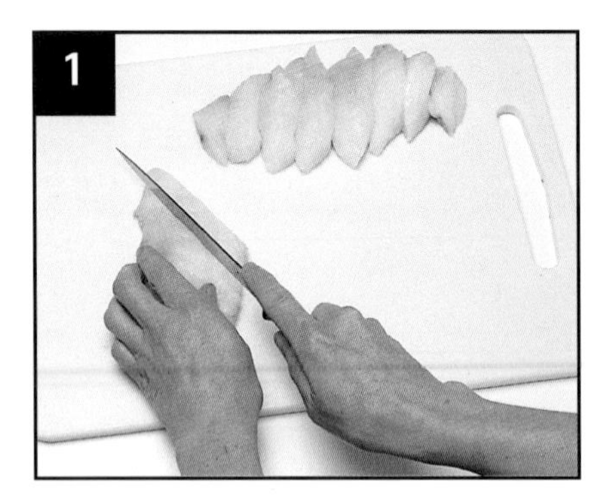
1

4

5

Salmon with Red Curry in Banana Leaves

Banana leaves are widely used in Thai cooking to wrap raw ingredients such as fish before baking or steaming. Oriental food shops usually stock them, but if you can't find any use foil or baking parchment.

Serves 4

INGREDIENTS

4 salmon steaks, about 175 g/6 oz each
2 banana leaves, halved
1 garlic clove, crushed
1 tsp fresh ginger root, grated
1 tbsp Thai red curry paste
1 tsp soft light brown sugar
1 tbsp Thai fish sauce
2 tbsp lime juice

TO GARNISH:
lime wedges
finely chopped red chilli

1 Place a salmon steak on the centre of each half banana leaf.

2 Mix together the garlic, ginger, curry paste, sugar and fish sauce. Spread this mixture over the surface of the fish and sprinkle with lime juice.

3 Wrap the banana leaves around the fish, tucking in the sides as you go to make a neat, compact bundle.

4 Place the parcels seam side down on a baking (cookie) sheet and bake in a preheated oven at 220°C/425°F/Gas Mark 7 for 15–20 minutes until the fish is cooked and the banana leaves are beginning to brown serve garnished with lime wedges and chilli.

COOK'S TIP

Fresh banana leaves are often sold in packs containing several leaves, but if you buy more than you need, they will store in the refrigerator for about a week.

Crispy Rice Noodles

This is a version of a favourite Thai dish, 'mee krob', one of those exciting dishes which varies from one household to another and one day to the next – depending on the ingredients available.

Serves 4

INGREDIENTS

vegetable oil for deep frying, plus 1½ tbsp
200 g/7 oz rice vermicelli noodles
1 onion, finely chopped
4 garlic cloves, finely chopped
1 boneless, skinless chicken breast (half), finely chopped
2 red bird-eye chillies, deseeded and sliced
4 tbsp dried black mushrooms, soaked and thinly sliced
3 tbsp dried prawns (shrimp)
4 spring onions (scallions), sliced
3 tbsp lime juice
2 tbsp soy sauce
2 tbsp Thai fish sauce
2 tbsp rice vinegar
2 tbsp soft light brown sugar
2 eggs, beaten
3 tbsp fresh coriander (cilantro), chopped
spring onion (scallion) curls, to garnish

1 Heat the oil in a large frying pan (skillet) or wok until very hot and deep-fry the noodles quickly, occasionally turning them, until puffed up, crisp and pale golden brown. Lift on to paper towels and drain well.

2 Heat 1 tablespoon oil and fry the onion and garlic for 1 minute. Add the chicken and stir-fry for 3 minutes. Add the chillies, mushrooms, dried prawns (shrimp) and spring onions (scallions).

3 Mix together the lime juice, soy sauce, fish sauce, rice vinegar and sugar, then stir into the pan and cook for a further minute. Remove the pan from the heat.

4 Heat the remaining oil in a wide pan and pour in the eggs to coat the base of the pan evenly, making a thin omelette. Cook until set and golden, then turn it over and cook the other side. Turn out and roll up, then slice into long ribbon strips.

5 Toss together the fried noodles, stir-fried ingredients, coriander (cilantro) and omelette strips. Garnish with spring onion (scallion) curls and serve at once.

1

2

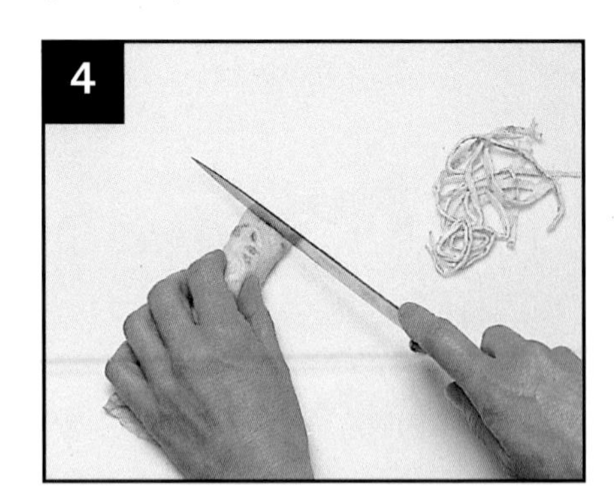
4

Hot & Sour Noodles

This simple, fast-food dish is sold from street food stalls in Thailand, with many and varied additions of meat and vegetables. It is equally good served hot or cold.

Serves 4

INGREDIENTS

250 g/9 oz dried medium egg noodles
1 tbsp sesame oil
1 tbsp chilli oil
1 garlic clove, crushed
2 spring onions (scallions), finely chopped
55 g/2 oz/$\frac{2}{3}$ cup button mushrooms, sliced
40 g/1$\frac{1}{2}$ oz/1 cup dried Chinese black mushrooms, soaked, drained and sliced
2 tbsp lime juice
3 tbsp light soy sauce
1 tsp sugar

TO SERVE:
shredded Chinese leaves
2 tbsp shredded coriander (cilantro)
2 tbsp toasted peanuts, chopped

1 Cook the noodles in a large pan of boiling water for 3–4 minutes, or according to the package directions. Drain well, return to the pan, toss with the sesame oil and set aside.

2 Heat the chilli oil in a large frying pan (skillet) or wok and quickly stir-fry the garlic, onions and button mushrooms to soften them.

3 Add the black mushrooms, lime juice, soy sauce and sugar and continue stir-frying until boiling. Add the noodles and toss to mix.

4 Serve spooned over Chinese leaves, sprinkled with coriander (cilantro) and peanuts.

COOK'S TIP

Thai chilli oil is very hot, so if you want a milder flavour, use vegetable oil for the initial cooking instead, then add a final dribble of chilli oil just for seasoning.

Pad Thai Noodles

The combination of ingredients in this classic noodle dish varies, depending on the cook, but it commonly contains a mixture of pork and prawns or other seafood.

Serves 4

INGREDIENTS

250 g/9 oz rice stick noodles
3 tbsp groundnut oil
3 garlic cloves, finely chopped
125 g/4½ oz pork fillet (tenderloin), chopped into 5 mm/¼ inch pieces
200 g/7 oz/1¼ cups prawns (shrimp), peeled
1 tbsp sugar
3 tbsp Thai fish sauce
1 tbsp tomato ketchup
1 tbsp lime juice
2 eggs, beaten
125 g/4½ oz/generous 1 cup beansprouts

TO GARNISH:
1 tsp dried red chilli flakes
2 spring onions (scallions), thickly sliced
2 tbsp fresh coriander (cilantro), chopped

1 Soak the rice noodles in hot water for about 15 minutes, or according to the package directions. Drain well and put to one side.

2 Heat the oil in a large frying pan (skillet) or wok and fry the garlic over a high heat for 30 seconds. Add the pork and stir-fry for 2–3 minutes until browned.

3 Stir in the prawns (shrimp), then add the sugar, fish sauce, ketchup and lime juice, and continue stir-frying for a further 30 seconds.

4 Stir in the eggs and stir-fry until lightly set. Stir in the noodles, then add the beansprouts and stir-fry for a further 30 seconds to cook lightly.

5 Turn out on to a serving dish and scatter with chilli flakes, spring onions (scallions) and coriander (cilantro).

COOK'S TIP

Drain the rice noodles before adding to the pan, as excess moisture will spoil the texture of the dish.

Drunken Noodles

Perhaps this would be more correctly named 'drunkards' noodles', as it's a dish that is supposedly often eaten as a hangover cure – the fiery kick of the chillies wakes up the system and the lime leaves and basil cleanse and refresh the palate.

Serves 4

INGREDIENTS

- 175 g/6 oz rice stick noodles
- 2 tbsp vegetable oil
- 1 garlic clove, crushed
- 2 small green chillies, chopped
- 1 small onion, thinly sliced
- 150 g/5½ oz lean minced (ground) pork or chicken
- 1 small green (bell) pepper, deseeded and finely chopped
- 4 kaffir lime leaves, finely shredded
- 1 tbsp dark soy sauce
- 1 tbsp light soy sauce
- ½ tsp sugar
- 1 tomato, cut into thin wedges
- 2 tbsp sweet basil leaves, finely sliced, to garnish

1 Soak the rice stick noodles in hot water for 15 minutes, or according to the package directions. Drain well.

2 Heat the oil in a wok and stir-fry the garlic, chillies and onion for 1 minute.

3 Stir in the pork or chicken and stir-fry on a high heat for a further minute, then add the pepper and continue stir-frying for a further 2 minutes.

4 Stir in the lime leaves, soy sauces and sugar. Add the noodles and tomato and toss well to heat thoroughly.

5 Sprinkle with the sliced basil leaves and serve hot.

COOK'S TIP

Fresh kaffir lime leaves freeze well, so if you buy more than you need, simply tie them in a tightly sealed polythene (plastic) freezer bag and freeze for up to a month. They can be used straight from the freezer.

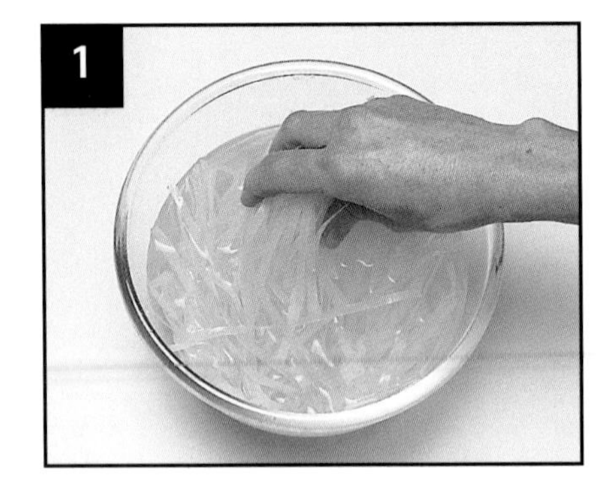
1

3

4

Jasmine Rice with Lemon & Basil

Jasmine rice has a delicate flavour and it can be served completely plain, with no other flavourings. This simple dish just has the light tang of lemon and soft scent of basil to add an extra touch.

Serves 4

INGREDIENTS

400 g/14 oz/2 cups jasmine rice
800 ml/28 fl oz/3½ cups water
rind of ½ lemon, finely grated
2 tbsp fresh sweet basil, chopped

1 Wash the rice in several changes of cold water until the water runs clear. Bring the water to the boil in a large pan, then add the rice.

2 Bring back to a rolling boil. Turn the heat to a low simmer, cover the pan and simmer for a further 12 minutes.

3 Remove the pan from the heat and leave to stand, covered, for 10 minutes.

4 Fluff up the rice with a fork, then stir in the lemon. Serve scattered with basil.

COOK'S TIP

It is important to leave the pan tightly covered while the rice cooks and steams inside so the grains cook evenly and become fluffy and separate.

Coconut Rice with Pineapple

Cooking rice in coconut milk makes it very satisfying and nutritious, and this is often used as a base for main dishes, with the addition of meat, fish, vegetables or eggs to make it more substantial.

Serves 4

INGREDIENTS

200 g/7 oz/1 cup long-grain rice
500 ml/18 fl oz/2¼ cups coconut milk
2 lemon grass stalks (stems)
200 ml/7 fl oz/scant 1 cup water
2 slices fresh pineapple, peeled and diced
2 tbsp toasted coconut
chilli sauce, to serve

1 Wash the rice in several changes of cold water until the water runs clear. Place in a large pan with the coconut milk.

2 Place the lemon grass on a firm work surface and bruise it by hitting firmly with a rolling pin or meat hammer. Add to the pan with the rice and coconut milk.

3 Add the water and bring to the boil. Lower the heat, cover the pan tightly and simmer gently for 15 minutes. Remove the pan from the heat and fluff up the rice with a fork.

4 Remove the lemon grass and stir in the pineapple. Scatter with toasted coconut and serve with chilli sauce.

VARIATION

A sweet version of this dish can be made by simply omitting the lemon grass and stirring in palm sugar or caster sugar to taste during cooking. Serve as a dessert, with extra pineapple slices.

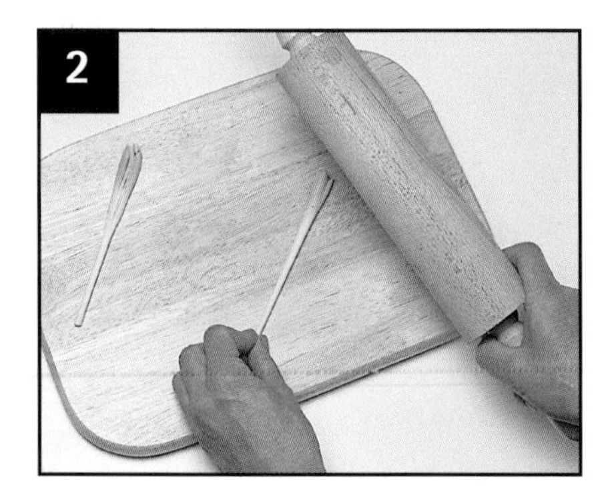